Salt in the City

by
'Funmi Adewole

Copyright Information

Text © 'Funmi Adewole Kruczkowska 2012 Collection under this cover © Kay Green 2013. All rights reserved. No part of this publication may be reproduced, stored in a retrieval system, rebound or transmitted in any form or for any purpose without the prior written permission of the author and publisher. This book is sold subject to the condition that it shall not be lent, resold, hired out or otherwise circulated without the publisher's prior consent in any form or binding other than that in which it is published.

Cover artwork based on a photo by Irven Lewis © 2013; Sleepwalker's dream photo © Simon Richardson.

Counterpoint first published in 'This is a book about Alice' pub Earlyworks Press 2013

Printed in the UK
by MPG Books Group

Paperback ISBN 9781906451-74-5
Ebook 9781906451-76-9

Published by Circaidy Gregory Press
Creative Media Centre
45 Robertson Street
Hastings, Sussex
TN34 1HL

www.circaidygregory.co.uk

Dedication

To my families

Contents

Acknowledgements and Introduction

Part one
Back Streets and Corridors

The fallacy of strife	1
No little girls grow	2
The heart's throb	3
Why write?	4
Thread-thin paths	5
Our feet possess the land	6
The snail	7
Mother's music	8
Anowa	9
Our poetry	11
A friend of the clime	12
The son	13
Memory and dream	14
Laughter	15
Sea salt in the city	16

Part two

Downtown

The matriarch	19
The abortive coup	20
The wall	21
The edifice	22
The refugee's brother	23
The wayfarer	25
The bereaved	28
Slaves of the heart beat	29
The rains	30
Untitled	31
Habitation	33
Counterpoint	37
Becoming	38
After that, then…	39
Index of first lines	43

Acknowledgements

Many thanks to fellow writers at the Poetry club of the University of Ibadan, Nigeria – you are the greatest of the greatest – and the Association of Nigerian Authors (ANA). Thanks to my lecturers Professor Dapo Adelugba, Professor Niyi Osundare and Professor Femi Osofisan for your encouragement. My appreciation to Dr Sola Olorunyomi and Professor Aderemi Raji-Oyelade (Remi Raji) for your passion for literature and generosity. Thank you John Paul O'Neil and Farrago poetry club, London for introducing me to Slam poetry and giving me my first professional spoken word gig.

A version of this collection *Sea-salt in the City* was runner-up in 1993 for The Association of Nigerian Authors (ANA) prize for unpublished manuscripts. The winner that year was Ogaga Ifowodo. My performance of *The wayfarer* won the Best Newcomer prize with the Farrago Poetry Club, London in 1998.

After that, then was first published in 2011 in *Seasons: The periodic journal of the international playwrights* (online) (www.seasonswomenplaywrights/2011/.../Afterthat-then).

The poems *No little Girls Grow, The Fallacy of Strife, The heart's throb* and *Sea-salt in the City* were first published in the anthology *Lagos of the Poets* (2010) edited by Odia Ofeimun. Odia, many thanks.

In 2008 with the support of the Arts Council England I developed *The Sleepwalker's Dream*, a short, movement-based performance based on extracts of poems. Space and feedback was provided by Caroline Salem, director of SPACE@Clarence Mews. The outcome was presented in the workshop performance programmes of the 2009 and 2010 *Beyond the Linear Narrative* Conferences at Goldsmith College, London (www.gold.ac.uk/pinter-centre/). It was also performed as part of the following:

- **Tales from other places,** a programme of solos by five women at Chisenhale dance space, 28 - 30 March 2008 at Chisenhale dance space   (chisenhaledancespace.co.uk) curated by Amy Voris, performed alongside solos by Tanya Mangalanayagam, Jo Dryer, Regula Voegelin and Amy Voris.

- **Spanning consciousness and continents,** an evening of solos connected by their exploration of psychological and cultural duality, 10 July 2009 at the Arcola theatre (arcolatheatre.com) as part of their *Create '09* season, curated by Cecile Feza Bushidi, performed alongside solos by Kweku Aacht and Cecile Feza Bushidi.

- **Local International,** 13 March 2010 at East London Dance (eastlondondance.org) as part of their *Dance Currents* season, curated by Kiki Gale, performed alongside Phoenix Dance Theatre, A-diaspora collective, Ballet Black and Yiphun Chiem.

Many thanks Caroline, Amy, Cecile and Kiki for believing in the piece.

Warm regards to the following organisations for great artistic experiences they provide: The Farrago Poetry (London.e-poets.net/about-farrago) Global Fusion Music and Arts (www.globalfusionarts.com), The Association of Dance of the African Diaspora (www.adad.org.uk), Numbi Arts (Numbi.org), SPACE@Clarence Mews (firth.salem@virgin.net), Don't Hit Mama (donthitmama.nl), Ecole des Sables (Jantbi.org) and Agape Productions Ltd (Agapeproductionsltd@gmail.com). Thank you Kay Green for your love of literature and the invitation to publish.

Appreciation to friends at Hillsong Church for 'doing life' with me. Big thanks to my sisters and brothers – Bunmi, Oyin, Gbenga, Yinka, and Leke for your love and support, to Mum, Monisola Cecilia Adewole (nee Ademiluyi) and Frances 'Mummy' Gander, (RIP) who as a little girl would ask me to send them poems with my letters. A big thank you to my Dad, Rufus Adewuyi Adewole for his recitations of Shakespeare at the dinner table. My husband Nick - Yes, let's! My stepson Joe – Bleee! To the Almighty, my gratitude and life.

Foreword

This collection is selected from poems I began to write in the mid-1980s when I was admitted to the University of Ibadan. I began writing poetry quite young, before I moved to Nigeria from England at the age of eight. With time, poetry became the space for working out my faith, relationships, the glimpses I was getting of a wider world, my struggles with learning Yoruba[1].

The university's poetry club provided great experiences. My poetry retained a personal edge but gained from a greater awareness of how the personal intersected with the political. I enjoyed the rhythm and the declamatory mode of the African poets that we studied such as Niyi Osundare and Okot p'Bitek. They infused literature with oral literature and seemed to situate the solo voice in the midst of the group. As the club's artistic director I had the opportunity to experiment with the performance of poetry, drawing inspiration from African storytelling conventions and Ntozake Shange's choreo-peom *For coloured girls who would have committed suicide when the rainbow was enuf.* I was also introduced to translations of Russian poetry, of Slyvia Plath and Emily Dickinson.

Political upheaval became increasingly common in the late 1980s, during the last years of my degree. After National Youth Service[2], I returned to Lagos where I started working in TV and radio. The media had just been privatised, up until then the media was state owned. Nollywood, the straight to video movie industry was taking off and outlets for magazine programmes and documentaries began

---

[1] *The Yoruba are a large West African ethnic group, now to be found mainly in Nigeria and Benin, with a well-documented cultural tradition.*

[2] *Nigerian graduates are expected to join the National Youth Service Corps, where they spend a year doing community service in a different part of the country to where they studied.*

to expand. The landscape shifted again after Sani Abacha[3] came to power. The City was a conundrum – ravaged by economic and political adversity – and yet full of promise and excitement. It was a time of chaos and thresholds.

I left for England in 1994 where I embarked on a career as a performer touring with dance, physical theatre and visual theatre companies. I found poetry again, this time in the overlap of fragments, genres and histories. I wrote the last three poems in the mid-2000s. With them I feel them this story is at last complete. Though not presented in strict chronological order, the earliest poems are at the beginning. I have rewritten *Anowa* and *A friend of the clime* but tried to maintain their original theme and character. I hope you enjoy the book.

'Funmi Adewole Kruczkowska, May 2012

---

[3] *Military ruler of Nigeria from 1993-1998. His rule was characterized by human rights violations and corruption.*

Sleepwalker's Dream – *a poetic review*

Funmi stands in a black silk slip
Face hyper animated below cropped Afro' hair
She taunts us then giggles
We're all invited to watch her play
While in with the bargain she tells us a story
Passing down the tales of the elders
Passionately delivered under stars
For this is the stuff of dreams
Sparks of the nocturnal
Red lights speak of internal worlds
Distorted by imagination
She stands in provocation
Manifestation of West African folklore
Spitting words of a by gone age
Interfacing with the present
Through mockery and disdain
A wash of amber
Late sun on red soil
Bare feet beating out
The rhythms of tradition
The sleepwalker runs in circles
Hurling towards oblivion
Before breaking down
And crashing to ground
Crisis over
Pull your self together
For there are more games to play
Stories to tell
Dances to dance
Til the distant glow of fire on the mountain
Emanates from moonlit magic

by Kweku Aacht – *Diarist in residence at East London Dance 2009/2010*

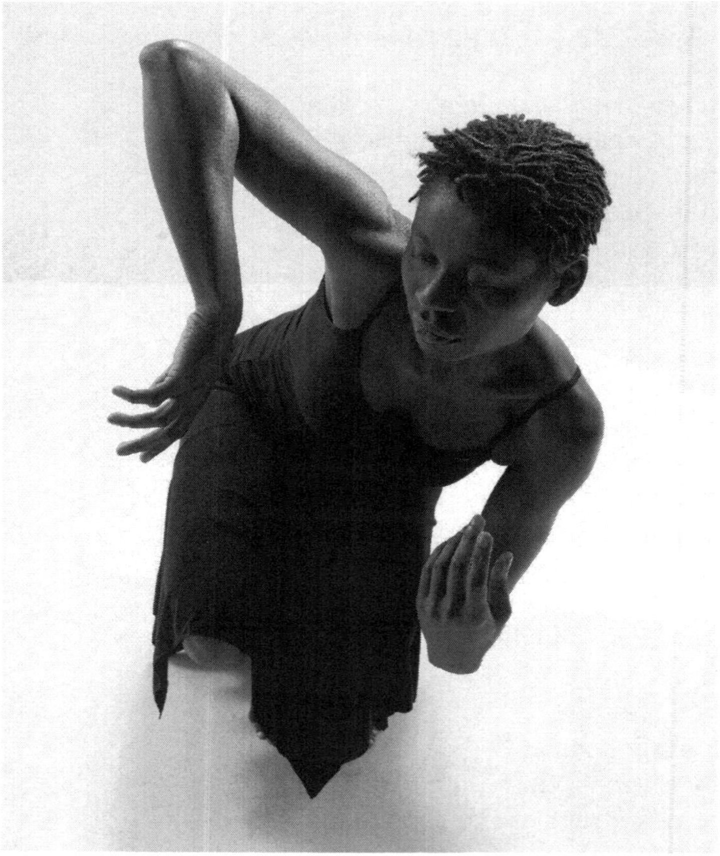

Sea Salt in the City

Part One

Back Streets and Corridors

The fallacy of strife

The soil lies fallow.
Have I not tilled the land enough?
Stretching from your soul into mine,
the wilderness is vast.

Life was once me
machete in hand, hitting the sand,
my angry heart planted chaos
sweat filled my face
like the sacrifice of Cain.

On barren land, nothing grows.

Only now that my arm is weak
nothing reveals herself.
I recognise her
in the puff of wind
and crumbling sand.

I know Nothing. I have known her for long.

I toil no more then.
The fallacy of strife stares hard at me.
The reflection in her eyes,
so mute and futile, is mine.

No little girls grow

The city?
I will not go there.
The inhabitants taunt
each other's helplessness
with stories of the Kurdistan babes
buried in the mountain peaks.
Such stories!
They are like rats
gnawing at the door
of my sanity.
I will not let them in.

The Kurdistan ghosts chatter persistently.
'This is a story that you must tell.'
'To whom?
To the City?'
I will not tell it.

But on the barren land
where fear has led me
no little girls grow.

Note:

Saddam Hussein attacked the Kurdish people on a number of occasions in the 1980s.

The heart's throb

Nothing makes the heart throb most
by clawing
groping paths
of yearning
Winding paths
that end up nowhere.

Fly
flee
continuously
Green hills, green trees
rush past spinning
Wait not
breathe not
for you will discover
at every
stop
corner
hiding place
you still meet with yourself.

Life revolves around activity
activity unceasing
unceasing activity
on and on
on, on and on
clink, clink glasses
bang, bop music.
Ha ha
Ho ho
Why?
What?
Move on, don't stop.
You will be left alone with yourself.

Why write?

Writing,
I sat alone in my room
hiding from the febrile darkness
of the night

but the night stares through my curtains
like Beanboy
his gaze marbled
with rejection.
The cold night returns
with the reminiscences
of Ratti,
in the wind
flap, flap, flapping my curtains with the rage
that ravaged through his veins
like fire in a forest on a harmattan day.
The curtains billow
full like mother's voice
sonorous with anxiety
echoing though the night
like the one
racking and breathless
Gifty froze
dead
still
still as this night
and Winifred's sobs
pitted our hearts
like the rain
patters my roof
this cold, windy, rainy night.
Why write? Why write?

Thread-thin paths

(for U.)

I tread thread-thin paths
that bind the sphere's
pain in one.
But the groaning clashes
of creation in conflict
infuse me with a panther-agility, still.
What then perturbs
the cherished steadiness of me?
Not the fiery thunders
of forces unknown
nor the pandemonium rising
with each new day.

Wait! Hear!
It's the coaxing call
Of a kindred spirit.
Come.
Walk on my path
for I will know
no other.

Our feet possess the land

The sky burnt.
I remember. Yes, even now
the flickers of blue and red
hot and lashing.
Tree warped in agony,
leaves contorted in livid pain
and I walked the bushes
through dankness so dense
I felt it with the palm of my hands.
And where were you?
Splashing in grey waters
spiralled by weeds, with slime
binding your back
The mirror in your hand wrapped
our world in its pupil and
revealed a sky of blue sapphire.
Trees were rhapsodic in the wind
and I was clad in woven silver.
You embodied the water
in the eye of the mirror

In a breath we entered the mirror
and smashed the glass at our heels.
Our feet possess the land.

The snail

Each word parades flippantly
in my mind
etched out of your terse response
to my monologuing.
    Your memory is antenna
        a snail's shell, a slug's foot

Through a protracted sunray
your face appears a bright shade
of rose petal. But it withers
at the slightest touch of a hand.
    Your memory is a snail's shell
        a slug's foot, a curse.

My eyes are widened
by the vision I have
of you a baby birthed
by a wolf's dark eye.

I return in hope
to this worn threshold
Let your memory
    be a firefly.

Mother's music

A hasty fist slams down
and a million pulverised mediations
permeate the air,
then nostrils, and mind
with a minute-long ecstasy

Music, strummed by mother's fingers
supports the lyrics of our songs
songs we sing behind locked doors
savouring our evanescent joys
tapping our feet in an unsure rhythm
on a dubious floor.

Anowa

My parents
set me by the rivers of Yebi
Sprouting suckling mothers
and proud male tillers of soil.
But I could not rest there.
My feet could not dance
to the drum beat
of my heart.
I escaped through
the forest to this coast
sprouting suckling mothers
and proud male traders of slaves.
But I cannot rest here
fruitless and shackled
the impotent man
with whom I faced
the fury of the forest.
The curses of slaves
pierce the sea breeze -
brush my cheek.
I squint at
Yebi shrouded by vows.
I sigh -
a glimpse of my mother's face.
I whisper farewell -
O! *mouth-that-eats-salt-and-pepper*.
I seek
a town, any town
sprouting suckling mothers
and proud male tillers of soil.
I take a path -
It runs and runs. It may never arrive.
My heart beat
drowns out

the crashing waves
the curses of slaves
My feet pound joyously, joyously
its drum beat
of dismay.

Note:

This poem is inspired by 'Anowa', a play by Ama Ata Adoo. It is set in the 1800s in what is now Ghana. Anowa elopes with a young man who later becomes involved in the slave trade. She is deeply troubled. The play ends with his suicide and her descent into madness.

Our poetry

Our poetry is still but perfume in the wind
though your tears have soothed my smarting fingers.
A ghost haunts our handclap
maims the leap of our song.
Foot those dusty paths
for the sake of the xylophone in our vision.
Smash the urn. I will caress the dust of cremated days
and rival taciturn spirits with transparent love

Voices like epitaphs spill
from pages of the past and gurgle
into my pensive ears.
'Ah!' I say, 'Music for my waiting feet
kindling for our dance of dreams.'
Now, my arms shall wreath every pain
that dared to rack you.

A friend of the clime

Night falls
noisily about us.
The river foams at the mouth
We scurry by in shock.

The ravaged child
that dwells in your eyes
incognito
grabs at my wrist, chuckling.

My one-legged stance
is mawkish, and hanging
like rags about me
is this dress of dreams.

The ring road wearies us
but we refuse the city ahead.
We count mileposts and toll gates,
another sun rise, another sun set.

We argue about Ahid and Bosnia's child
rehearsing our contradictions
like echoes in the wilderness. We are tossed
together by the clime.

The son

The sun streaks the sky
Like a thunder clap.

I alight
On an iron horizon.

The vast sea
shrouds the shipwreck.
Waves bear a wreath of seaweed.

Above,
the expanse is filled with stepping clouds
- solid, firm for the feet.

The Son is beckoning me.

And beneath the waves
the rot
fertilizes the now.

Memory and dream

"Remember the house from where you come:
the cold floor, the childish laughter in the corridor.

Ask your friend, Memory

Hands opened like beggar's bowls
Within the empty room called home.

And little fingers searched across
The black stare of its walls."

"Yes, I remember
But the road is beyond the household wall

I trust more my friend Dream,

And now I must go and find her
before, like a sun-ray,

she disappears
With the advancing dusk."

Laughter

Laughter has shown me a way:

step out into the vastness.

Where these twelve roads meet
is Redemption.

Step out and study
the emptiness of your hands.

This is life; this is laughter.

Sea-salt in the city

Hot winds of woe sweep the street
The child smells the sea from the city dust-heap
The mother smells the muck at their feet.

Hot whispers of woe fill the head
of the old man in the run-down shed.
In the sea-shell on his window ledge
waves tumble, free.

Hot winds of woe sweep the street.
The parents, the priest, the prostitute
scream: why?

The pained dog's bark is a lullaby
and the child sinks into the sea of sleep

Hot winds of woe sweep the street
yet sea-salt rides these currents to the city.

Sea Salt in the City

Part Two

Downtown

The matriarch

Your creaseless face is a picture
of my days, when days were days for dreaming
when in the tin-top villas, ablaze like your body,
I discovered in piecemeal, in praise-songs
in the shadows of waning women
the hide that makes good drum,
the fire that ignites the drummer.

From the welcomes and whispers of wives, I gleaned
the potency to tread the revered ways,
ways away from the sighs of my mother
sighs that ushered me out house;
followed me outback; haunted my soul.
The journey to Lagos jostled in the mammy-wagon
and halted at her grave. The journey jostled
like your wide-hipped walk
The rhythm of the drum; the fire of the drummer.

*

Your creaseless face is my master plan
the plot for my return.

The abortive coup

The streets jostled with vacant faces
in the drabness of Oshodi market
where the *alakara* sang, and guns boomed
and from the break of day
the radio declaimed the same refrain.

As she wrapped her wares in the president's picture
she said life itself is a song.

"Our lives are but variants of the same tune
so leave me to write my young ones' lyrics
with the inky sweat of my ready mind.
Guns may boom from the nearby barracks
but my children dance the rhythms that I choose."

Note: An alakara is a bean cake-seller.

The wall

He lunges, and dents
her soul – quietly.
She fills up.
The World is now open
to another reading.

She watches wide-eyed
as ghostly corridors materialize.

She can pause in them,
dissect her gait; perform post-mortem
on the fabric
twitching her thigh.

In awe she beholds her body:
dust and dress an edifice.
She tinkers with its archetype.

A confusing form picks
at his face. He is
aghast, the mould
drops from his jaw.

Her scorn is breezy
her question – the wall.

The edifice

Pain is astray in this edifice
of musty rooms and lost keys.

The lady of the house
tends her Greek garden
in the racy pace of Lagos city.

Beguiled by the aroma
of her corridor's potted trees
we forgot the broken back door.

We artisans left the lady
watching over her backyard
with eyes of longing,
ears of expectation.

The refugee's brother

The smells of grilled fish and suya
waft into his hotel room.
The masquerade is dancing
the flash bulbs are popping.

The letter from his brother
Says he is a happy refugee.

Unhappily he observes the crowd:
The kimonoed lady
bound but beautiful
standing next to the cowboy hat.

His placard snaps.

He weeps, struggling to manage
the gap between Vision and Dream.
Blinded by migraines
he seeks the new order
in the campaign files
on his cluttered desk. The wind

is like a mischievous child at the curtain.
Again, fish and exotica waft in
again, the drumbeat. The masquerade flies
to – the tourist
and fro – his stare.
The lady in kimono gasps
The white man in the cowboy hat
growls back. The masquerade circles. The children clap.

What artefacts define the shape of his being awake?

The torn letter
The kimono's crease
The cowboy's hat
Drummer's beat.

The wayfarer
(For D.)

The wayfarer asked the trickster
to number the hermit's desert home
and his face, wrinkling by his oasis
calm, resigned, waiting.

The trickster intoned the lines of Beckett.

The wayfarer pointed at
the strong man, mid-crowd,
angry on the fringes of the dark.
"He knows how to challenge the overlords."

So a milestone hence where the blood-splattered magnificence
of the city stood, there

the trickster engraved the manifesto.

To the bars of the backstreets
roaming like the Iliad
they traversed the city together,
found it full of comrades like them
calm, resolute, wanton.

Wanton, they emptied their gourds
into their bellies, drowsy
in the soberness of eventide.
Tomorrow is always furious.

The trickster shared out the opium.

With the heat of their depths
the skies redden.
It blurred their bitter gaze, swamping
its link with

the violent and ignominious in the back streets,
sheathing their daggers at the crack of dawn.
The conundrums filling the sanctuaries,
rejecting salvation but seeking succour.

The trickster's laughter was a eulogy

to the mountains, so they ascended those
mute, motionless witnesses of time
(Not minutes or hours but breath.
To hold back time is death.)

Whilst the wayfarer surveyed the mountain view.
The trickster turned to turned to her and said

"Black woman, hips wide as the middle passage,
the wrath of your ancestors
demands sacrifice of you.

Cosmopolitan gutter child of forgotten genealogy
wear your grandmother's waist beads and
chant her praise in your search for identity

Sight without seeing is no mystery
Worship without God is no mystery
The mountains know no mysteries.

You run like dye in the cheap cloth
of your politick, doped by the mountain's trick
which glorifies your city's dumps.

From your mother's womb
you have chanted after me
rejoicing in impish victories,
creating greater challenges for your children.

Know your daily routine.
It utters deep lies.
You have no home to return to."

The bereaved
(For L.)

In the moment his mother died
he realised she had been living.
He wrapped her in a linen shroud
and elders arose
demanding blessings from his hands.
His benevolence was broken
over her gravestone. Mourners' smirks knifed him.
His end was not swift. He struggled
to stop his innocence from slipping away.
But slowly, slowly
the secret
of her life
overcame him.

Slaves of the heart beat

Castles do not quake at the nimble advance
of tiny feet.
The soil is but slightly grazed
but surely eroded.

The moon throbs through the thicket of foliage
hiding the sky
like a promise of today through
an oblique present.

Knuckles burst their sheathing
ripping bush paths through the thistle,
like corn through a furrow.

At twilight
and dawn no one sees the tears
on tiny cheeks
(and the noon-day sun dries them up)
nor the crimson fingers
working like spider legs
weaving an unsurpassable web
in silken threads of moonbeam and blood.

They slave under the beatings
of a thousand hearts in
thunderous unison.

The rains

The songs pour down
streets are submerged
water seeps under heavy *iroko* doors.
The river comes lapping feet and furniture
again, again
like unflinching laughter.
As ears tune the songs
feet begin to wade
hibiscus and stories
dance naked out of bodies.
The beat, the beat
so spare, primordial
unashamed
us.
These songs
because the seasons
are too nimble for the city.
Backstreet of our wider life
                so subtle
                so slight
                the line
                between
                the hibiscus
                and pain.
Ours are the deep northern ballads
Ours are the latter *rains*.

Note:
The iroko is a large tree, similar to an oak

Untitled

The red samurai and the bondwoman's son
on either side of the chosen ones
cupping their woes
weave their destinies into one.
In the Isles a million sigh
as Ham rises to salute the cross-bearing Cyrene.
Jo'burg is robed in pink
Magog is active
Radio active
and the surfeited dance doom
along beaches
among missiles.
Up the skyscrapers of Washington
A red button is hidden
in a white house.
Ozone stalks the Mexican thoroughbreds.
All power to the nations?

Birth, life, death are like the mesh
on the wrong side of the embroidered cradle-cloth.

Come, wash your hands.

Time and this newborn babe
are thoughtless.

Come, eat with me.

You have laboured and
your husband was slain in mid-stride.

We do not know why.

Sometimes the seasons are talkative
sometimes the seasons are terse.

Come, rest in my arms.

Embedded is the thread that strings the days
to the faces of men.

Come, rest.

Your baby growing in the beauty of that cloth
will decipher both sides of its pattern.

Rest.

Habitation

(i)
Mixed in the cup of libation
was the sweat of a million faces.
Trudging through the Badagry sand,
the blood of a salt-starved Biafran baby
and the pus of a Broad Street beggar.
What covenant have we made over the land?
Whose landmarks have we moved?
Exhume the bodies in the market place.
The spectacle is enough to tell us.

(ii)
Around us the billboards tower
blocking out sun.
We trim our lamps and listen
to waves of prophecy
washing the beach.

Washing over this city is the ocean
where oysters pearl and salt preserves.

With mouth white with salt
I can sing

but a sad song.

(iii)
The singing corpse of a breastless woman
straddles the road to our nationhood.
We sought for the centre of our land
but instead found a counter
where a multitude casts cowries
and mouths the pledge like a lame incantation.

A cashier humming plantation songs
sprinkles white ash on the multitude
and a truce overcasts the sky.

The song of the spectacular
corpse fills the air:

"Show me your face
And I will smash your god."

Now, a different colour of suicide
occurs each hour after Curfew.

(iv)
The Curfew calls
the Sunlight a liar, the sun's light a lie.

The Night, bare and stupendous, promising nothing, asks
'What is an inner song to the horror of Esau's hunger?'

The Light never
ceases it parables:

Since the world is an uncomfortable womb
is not Death, but a birth pang?
If you must remain a child, why and what is youth?

(v)
Love with His tenacious hand
and far seeing-eye
is the Sun-storm.

The Storm: hailstones of Sun-light
ravage the dunes of grey existence.

Bivouacked under opaque skies
We twist, vomit, arise.

Peace is a spoil of war.

Our tangled memories are snipers.
The frontline is a sigh.

(vi)
Peace is a dangerous word
to utter in the face of the multitude
but when we heard it
the storm quelled in our bellies

So let us say it
in the hearing of the taskmaster
in the very ears of the truce makers.

Let us say it
over the grave of the old man
making the diviners mad.

Let us
defy the absence of arable dwellings.
Spirits are fertile

This word is seed
it will bud. It will tree
and be shade for
habitation.

Counterpoint
(A memory of an Afro-beat queen)

To my child's eyes
she was from another dimension.
Her spotted face like a leopard
her insolent mouth, glazed.
as she passed, people whispered
War. Rape. Barren. Worthless. Debased.
but meeting her gaze, all accusers blushed.
Men and women, all, hushed.

She cursed. I shuddered,
and she called my shudder
dance.

My child's mind
toyed with her contradictory gait.
She, circling the street, both hunter and prey
she, listening for voyeurs to intimidate
she, a counterpoint
to the dissonant, dusty roads at curfew.
I tiptoed behind her. She cursed.
I fled away.

She turned and laughed
and called my fragmented flight
dance.

Becoming

Suddenly all my anxieties collapsed upon me
my shelter of busyness destroyed by tiny actions
of listening, breathing and resting in bed.
After raging against the absurdities that engender our respect
of open spaces, I was no more afraid. So
no longer loiter between Time and Eternity, my brother.
The blood of Christ is here. I have lost my rights to hatred
and I am home, as is Ibidun, the disdained
feasting with the Godhead. And we are all precious
as the hacked up bodies of fleeing Rwandans are precious
as the amputees of the Angolan mines are precious
as you are precious my Caucasian brother,
driven by the deeds of your ancestors like chaff
across the plains of India. You float back, confused,
to your white-collar job and the affirmation of me
meeting you for a pizza in the city.
To your complaint that Italians do not cook pizza with
pineapple, I say:
'Peace. Be still. Aren't your taste buds rejoicing?'
In Time, History lives in the green room.
In Eternity, She takes to the stage. So
let us continue then, on this slow road called Becoming,
His blood on our faces
and all over our means forever more.

After that, then

I had forgotten what Eternity was like,
loitering as I was at the door posts of Time.
I had forgotten Eternity because Time is so much louder.
The force of Time is the force of realisation. Eternity
is subtle. She moves silently in spheres
Time moves sharply like arrows
piercing the heart.

My mother told me in the space of my lifetime
she squashed my grandfather's coronation, her father's festivities
several farmsteads and hope.
Crystallised by ritual into two two bedroom flats
in Lagos and London, south of the river – the reason
ghosts pressed against the windowpanes
beckoning me beyond the balconies
only to fall silent when I reached the edge. Anyhow

the legacies and genealogies are now written.
No more fear of forgetting them. No more need
of remembering them. Empire becomes hamlet, becomes highway.
Highway becomes hallway. The morphing landscape
from this majestic moutain view
spans Benin, Rome, Mali, Samaria, all.

The sun is rising above our garden. Let us have breakfast.
After that we will take a walk. Then we will work. Then
we will help each other. After that we will ease ourselves.
Then we will sing and dance and worship. We will laugh and
chat. Then sleep.
After that, then…

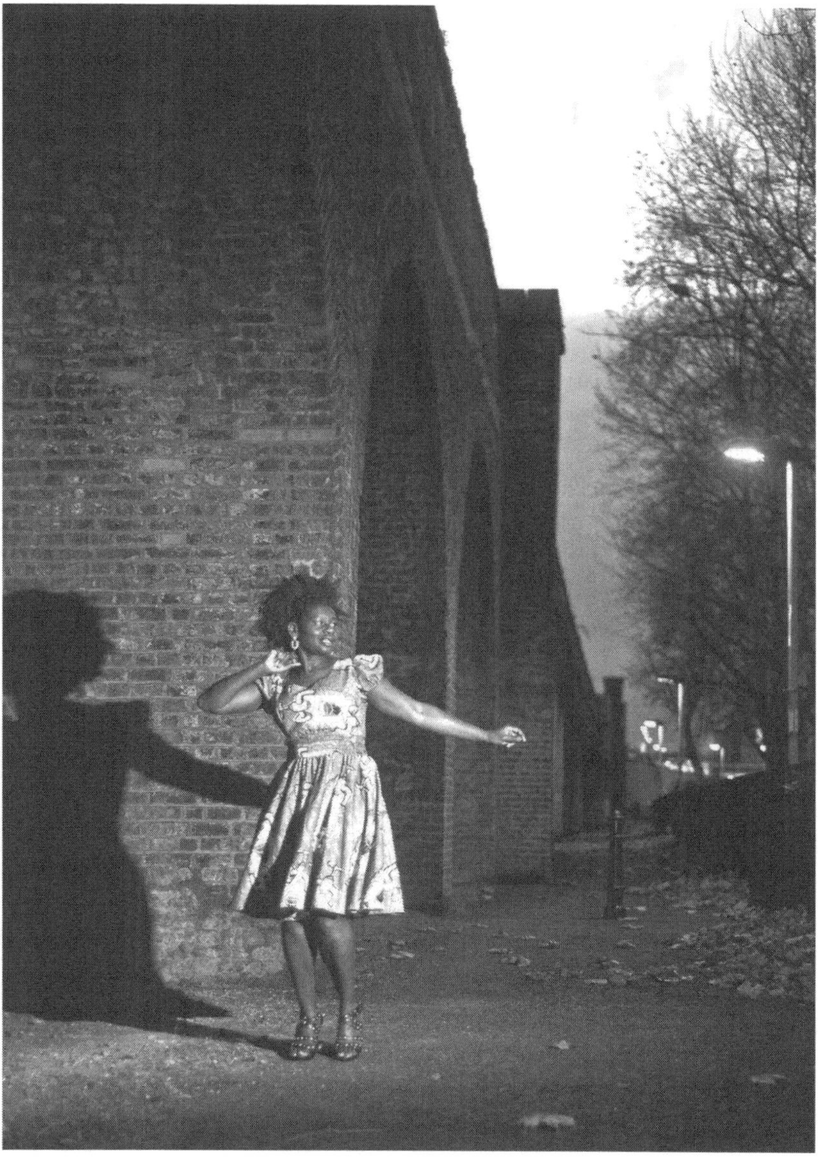

Index of First Lines

Castles do not quake at the nimble advance	29
city?, The	1
Each word parades flippantly	7
hasty fist slams down, A	8
He lunges, and dents	21
Hot winds of woe sweep the street	16
I had forgotten what Eternity was like,	39
I tread thread-thin paths	5
In the moment his mother died	28
Laughter has shown me a way:	15
Mixed in the cup of libation	33
My parents	9
Night falls	12
Nothing makes the heart throb most	3
Our poetry is still but perfume in the wind	11
Pain is astray in this edifice	22
red samurai and the bondwoman's son, The	31
"Remember the house from where you come:	14
sky burnt., The	6
smells of grilled fish and suya, The	23
soil lies fallow, The	1
songs pour down, The	30

streets jostled with vacant faces, The	20
Suddenly all my anxieties collapsed upon me	38
sun streaks the sky, The	13
To my child's eyes	37
wayfarer asked the trickster, The	25
Writing, I sat alone…	4
Your creaseless face is a picture	19